D1259105

JANE LONG
"Mother of Texas"

JANE LONG
"Mother of Texas"

JANE LONG

The Mother of Texas

by
Catherine Troxell Gonzalez

EAKIN PRESS ★ AUSTIN, TEXAS

FIRST EDITION
Second Printing

Published in the United States of America
By Eakin Publications, Inc.,
PO. Box 23066, Austin, Texas 78735

ISBN 0-89015-299-3

INTRODUCTION

Known as the "Mother of Texas", Jane Wilkinson Long was the first known woman of English descent to enter Texas and bore the first known child of Anglo-American parents in the state. Although born in Maryland, she moved with her mother to Natchez, Mississippi, after the death of her father. A chance meeting and a quick romance led to her marriage with Dr. James Long in 1815.

A daughter was born to the Longs in 1816 and another in 1819. With this infant of two weeks, the older daughter, Ann, and a Negro servant, Mrs. Long left Natchez, travelling up Red River through Louisiana, to overtake her husband, who had gone to Texas on an expedition. She was delayed, however, by illness and had to remain four weeks at the home of her sister in Alexandria, Louisiana.

After her recovery, Mrs. Long left the infant (who soon died), and pushed on to join her husband at Nacogdoches, Texas. Forced by the Spanish to flee from Nacogdoches, Jane later rejoined her husband and returned to Louisiana.

In 1820 the Longs came by boat to Bolivar Point near Galveston where James Long was organizing another expedition to make Texas a republic. During the bitter winter of 1821, while her husband was gone, Jane, her servant Kian, and daughter, Ann, spent miserable months awaiting Gen. Long's return, much of the time without proper food and fuel. During this time another daughter, Mary James, was born. Shortly thereafter, Mrs. Long learned of the death of her husband in Mexico.

In 1827 Jane received title to land in present-day Waller County, and in later years operated a boarding house at Brazoria. She finally sold this and opened a hotel at Richmond. She died there in 1880. Jane Long was acquainted with many of the earliest settlers of Texas, as well as many of the prominent historical figures found in Texas history.

Stories

For Young

Americans

I

Young Jane

Jane heard the slam of a door in the back of the big house. Then suddenly she could hear the voice of Kian, shouting with glee.

"Come on, Miss Jane," the young Negro girl urged her. "You jes gotta see this young gentlemun!"

"Kian, stop it. I have to go back to school. I don't have time for any more of your foolishness. Go wash your hands and straighten your apron," the young lady ordered.

"But, Miss Jane, you jes oughter see 'im. He's jes the prettiest thing you ever seen," Kian kept pushing at Jane.

"Oh, all right, but I have to hurry or I'll be late," answered Jane.

"He's right upstairs with that sick soldier. He'll be coming back down in a few minutes. Don't go 'way, thouht you see 'im," cried the eager Kian.

Jane Wilkinson had owned her young slave, Kian, for a long time now. She knew Kian wouldn't be fussing so much unless the young man was really nice. But, after all, Jane had many young men who wanted her friendship. At seventeen, Jane was a beautiful girl, long dark curls and flashing eyes. Many admirers came to the plantation just to enjoy the sunshine of her smile.

However, she must not be late back to her school. The headmaster had warned her just yesterday about being tardy at lunch. Jane pulled at the ribbons of her shiny, green poke bonnet. The satin ruffles framed her smiling face.

"All right, Kian," she answered. "I'll wait for a few minutes."

"Missy, you shore won't be sorry you waited!" Kian vowed. She stood proudly, watching Jane. Kian was not about to miss this meeting. She wanted her young mistress to share her own pleasure in seeing this handsome young man. Besides, it was her idea for Jane to meet him. She loved Jane with all her heart.

A soft breeze blew in through the wide front door. Jane pinched her cheeks. She rubbed at her lips as she gazed into the mirror on the hat rack. She tapped her foot on the wide oak floor. Waiting was not a thing Jane liked to do.

Her eyes turned toward the wide stairway. There was the sound of a door opening at the head of the stairs. From it came a tall, handsome young man. He was about twenty-two.

He smiled as he came down the stairs. At the bottom he spoke to Jane. She held out her hand, and he bowed low over it. He kissed her hand and then let it go.

"I'm Jane Wilkinson," she said. "I live here at Propinquity with my sister and brother-in-law."

"I am very happy to meet you, Miss Jane," the young man answered. "It is a pleasure to find one so beautiful and charming."

He stared at Jane until she blushed. He could not take his eyes off this lovely young lady. Her dark curls framed her creamy white face.

At last Jane remembered her manners.

"Won't you sit in the parlor?" she invited him. She wasn't sure it was proper, but Jane didn't worry about that now. They chose a place near the wide bay window. The game board was open between the two chairs. It was not long before they were busy with a game of checkers.

James Long thought fast. He bet Jane that he could beat her. Then he proposed that the forfeit be a pair of gloves. With skill he managed to lose the game without Jane's being aware of his plan.

As he left the house, he reminded Jane that he would return the next day. He came early in the afternoon with a lovely pair of gloves.

"But, sir, I cannot accept them. It would be a gaming debt," said Jane. She knew that her sister would not like her accepting the gloves from a stranger.

"Well, then, perhaps you can accept them as a gift," he answered with ease.

Jane objected for a few minutes, but then she took the gloves and began slipping them on her fingers. She glanced up at him from under her long lashes.

"Now, then," James continued, "won't you give me the hand that my gift fits so well?"

The blush became deeper on Jane's face. "You're teasing me, sir," Jane said. A tinkling little laugh followed her words.

But James Long was not teasing. He laid his plans well for his courtship of young Jane. It was clear to everyone that he was in earnest. He found every excuse for visiting the plantation, even after his patient had recovered.

Jane Wilkinson had lived the life of a sheltered young daughter of well-to-do Southern parents. She had been born in Clark County, Maryland, in 1798.

Jane's father had died about a year after she was born. Her mother moved with her family to the Mississippi Territory when Jane was fifteen. They had been in the territory only a year when Jane's mother died. After her mother's death, Jane went to live at Propinquity Plantation with her sister, Barbara Wilkinson Calvit.

"Barbara," the mother had told her older daughter as she lay dying, "take good care of my baby. She's so stubborn and headstrong. She needs guidance. Don't let her run wild. She's so young to be alone."

Tears streamed down Barbara's face as she answered her mother, "I'll be a mother to her. Don't worry, please, Mother, I'll take good care of her."

True to her promise, Barbara did try to take good care of her little sister. Barbara remembered that promise when young Dr. Long came to ask for Jane's hand in marriage. Jane was entirely too young to be married. Barbara shook her head firmly. She and her husband would not agree to let Jane marry this young man. Dr. James Long was a fine young man, but he was too eager and ambitious. They feared his love of adventure might take Jane away from them.

Jane stamped her foot in anger. "I will marry him. I love James and he loves me," she shouted. But she knew that she would have to have her sister's permission. There just had to be some way that they could be married.

Jane fretted for days. She considered running away, but James would not even discuss that. Anyway, the Calvits would just bring her back to Propinquity. She and James discussed the problem at length. James tried to tell her that he would wait until she was old enough. But Jane did not want to wait.

"James, I love you. I want to share all of your life. I don't want to wait until I am an old lady," cried Jane.

4

"Well, Jane, there is a way," James told her. He was hesitant about explaining it to Jane. After all, she was so very young. But he too loved Jane and wanted her for his wife at once. Surely, the Calvits would agree when they saw how serious the young lovers were.

"James, what is it?" Jane demanded. She felt that every moment of their future was precious. James' slowness drove her mad. Her youth made her so impatient.

"You see, Jane, you are an orphan. There is a law here in the Mississippi Territory. An orphan can choose his own guardian. You can make that choice. You don't have to choose the Calvits as they expect you to do. I can be your guardian. Then we can be married at once," James told her.

A big smile covered Jane's face. The problem was solved for her. She could have her James right away. There could be no objection now.

When she informed the Calvits of her decision, they were furious. But there was nothing they could do. Jane would have her way after all. The impetuous young Dr. Long would be her husband.

They were married May 14, 1815, and went to live on Dr. Long's plantation, Walnut Hills, near Natchez, Mississippi. The estate business took much of his time. He gave up his practice of surgery. The young couple spent two very happy years at Walnut Hills. It was on this plantation that their first child, Ann Herbert Long, was born.

In spite of all the happy times, James Long thought often of his life as a soldier. The world of adventure called to him. He remembered the times with Andrew Jackson in the Battle of New Orleans. Jackson had called him "My young Lion." James Long became restless on the plantation. He felt the call of danger and excitement.

Jane knew his state of mind. She tried to keep him occupied with affairs of business on the plantation. All her efforts were in vain.

"Jane, there is a whole big world out there to be conquered," James told her. "I want to do something important in my life. All the West is ours for the taking. The Spanish can't hold all that huge Texas land with their slim forces. We can make it another territory of the United States like Mississippi. I know we can do it."

"But James, you have already done your share. You fought in New Orleans to hold this territory," Jane answered. "You can't keep on fighting all of your life."

"I can, too, Jane. I want us to have more land than this one plantation. We can have thousands of acres of good Texas land," he told her. "Philip Nolan led a filibuster into Texas. There is fabulous wealth there. I know I can do it!"

All Jane's pleas came to nothing. About this time an expedition to Texas was planned. General Adair of Kentucky was to be its leader. But General Adair was unable to complete the mission. It was offered to James Long. Excitedly, he accepted the challenge. Long even invested his entire fortune in the project.

James Long was filled with his plans. He could talk of nothing else. He would go from Natchez to Nacogdoches. There he would establish his headquarters. From that point he would be able to move into Texas. Anything that seemed to delay him made James fret.

Jane's happy life was over. She would have to give in to this husband of hers. The Calvits, Barbara and Alexander, were quick to point out her mistake in the early marriage. However, they did not let their disapproval of James upset Jane's plans. They offered to care for her and Ann while James was gone to Texas.

But Jane Long was not to be reckoned with. She had made up her mind to follow James into Texas. If he would not let her go with him, then she would be right behind him. It did not matter to her that she was soon to have a second child. Just as quickly as that baby was born, Jane and the two children would set out for Texas. The stubborn young Jane, whom her mother had begged Barbara to protect, was determined.

James begged her to be reasonable. "But Jane, you can't go to that wild, rugged country with two babies," he told her.

"Well, I won't let you go without me," she answered. "If you don't take me, I'll follow you."

"Jane, listen to me, for once!" he stormed. "I will send after you as soon as I can build a place for you to stay."

"It had better be quick," she answered. "I will not stay away from you for long."

The matter seemed settled. Jane plunged into the plans for the expedition. She and her sister made a flag for the new republic. James Long had designed it. It was made of white silk. There was a white star in the upper left corner placed upon a background of red. Red stripes were sewn across the white flag. Thus was born the Lone Star flag of Texas.

Dr. Long had seventy-five men enlisted in his company. They left Natchez amid much excitement and fanfare. Along the way to Nacogdoches they picked up enough recruits to bring the force to three hundred men. At Nacogdoches General Long took possession of an old stone fort, where he raised the first Lone Star flag over Texas. Texas was officially declared a republic.

Twelve days after Long left Natchez, Jane completed her plans. The second baby was born. Without waiting to regain her health, Jane with Kian and the two babies made her way to the river below Natchez. There she hired a boat to take her as far as Alexandria, Louisiana, where the Calvits had moved. Before she could leave, however, Jane was approached by a young man who had recognized her.

"Jane Long, what are you doing in this part of town?" the young man inquired. Then he saw her luggage. He knew without further questions what she was planning to do.

"Just leave me alone, Mr. Rowan. I know what I'm doing," Jane told him. "I am going to join my husband in Texas."

"But, Mrs. Long, you can't take two babies into that wilderness! There are difficult swamps, mud, and rain. You'll die in this weather," the young man told her. He felt that he had to persuade her not to go. She knew nothing about this kind of travel. The life would certainly be too hard for her.

"I can endure anything, if I can just go to my husband," Jane replied stubbornly. "I must go with him wherever he goes."

Knowing that she was determined to go, James Rowan decided to help her. He made arrangements for the captain of a small river boat to take care of her. Then, afraid for her safety, he made up his mind to go with her. He could help her get to her sister's home in Alexandria. Perhaps there they could talk her out of going further.

As Rowan had warned her, the trip was long and hard. They stopped often for wood and water. They took on other passengers. The quarters for Jane, Kian, and the babies were small and hot. Finally, the boat was caught on a sand bar in the river. The captain told them that he could go no further.

James Rowan sent ahead for horses to get them to Alexandria. After several days' wait, a young man arrived with two horses. Jane and Kian rode one horse. James Rowan mounted the other, carrying the baby in his arms. Little Ann Herbert Long rode behind him.

It was twenty days after she had left Natchez that Jane Long arrived in Alexandria. She was sick, tired, but not discouraged. She still intended to get to her husband's headquarters in Nacogdoches. But what she had not counted on happened. Jane Long was seriously ill. The trip had been too much for the young woman. Her sister, Barbara Calvit, put her to bed with a high fever.

"Jane, this trip is madness," Barbara told her. "You cannot go on with your plans. You will die if you continue to travel in this condition."

"Barbara, dear Barbara," Jane answered. "I know you mean well, but as soon as I get better, I must be on my way to James."

"James expects you to take care of yourself and these babies," Barbara answered her swiftly. She was determined that Jane must give up her plan. This traveling was nonsense.

However, Jane continued to make her plans, even as she lay dangerously ill. She was forced to stay with the Calvits for a month. Slowly, she recovered enough to make more plans for travel.

James Rowan stayed in Alexandria for another week. Then after urging her to drop her idea for going to Texas, he made her promise to wait until she was stronger. He arranged for her trip. He lent her money. He also gave her a letter of credit on his bank in Natchez. He did everything he could to make her way comfortable. Then he had to leave for his home in Natchez. Business wouldn't wait for him to go all the way to Texas.

Jane remained in Barbara's home for a month. Finally, the doctors decided that part of her illness was caused by her desire to see her husband. Even though they could not say that she was well, they made up their minds to let her go on. It seemed that she would die if she had to stay in Alexandria without James. Thus she was able to go on with her travel.

Jane learned that a group of men were leaving Alexandria to join her husband. It was with this party that she decided to travel. Randall Jones, her husband's friend, agreed to go with her. Jane bought a carriage, stocked food for the trip, and arranged to leave the baby with Barbara Calvit. Taking Ann and Kian with her, Jane told her sister good-bye. At last she was off on her journey to her husband.

Barbara placed her arms around the thin and worn Jane. "Try to take care of yourself, Jane. We love you and wish you well on this trip. Come back to us when you can," she told her sister.

"Barbara, just take care of my little baby. I'll be back for her when I can," Jane answered, as she handed the baby to her sister.

Jane joined Kian and Ann in the carriage. Randall Jones rode beside the carriage. The others in the party followed behind. At last, Jane thought, I shall see my beloved husband again. She closed her eyes, letting her mind carry her forward to that meeting.

The trip to Natchitoches was without trouble. They arrived there in a few days' time. It was here that Jane met her cousin, Captain Biddle Wilkinson. The party rested several days. Then they started out again toward Nacogdoches.

Travel became more difficult. The rains delayed them. The trails were rough, and the carriage bogged down in the mud many times.

"Mr. Jones, do you think we'll ever get there?" Jane asked. "Do you think that James has gotten my letter? I know he'll be at the Sabine to meet us."

Indeed James Long did receive her message. He hurried to the Sabine River to meet his wife. But the rains had delayed her party so much that he could not wait. He left word with the man who ran the ferry.

"Tell my wife that I had an urgent message to return. I shall wait for her at Nacogdoches," Long told James Gaines, the ferry operator.

"I'll tell her the minute she arrives," Gaines promised him. "We'll take good care of your family."

James Long, who by this time had earned the title General Long, left the river, secure in the knowledge that his wife would soon be with him.

It was at this point that Jane decided to make the rest of the trip without the carriage. They would ride mules to Nacogdoches. In spite of this faster method, they made only seven miles the next day. They spent the night at the home of a Mr. Early. The following day they rode out in the rain. It continued to rain on them all day. Jane shivered with the chilling rain.

Long after dark that night, they saw a light. They were at the Alexander home on the Attoyac River. Again Jane was chilled and wet to the bone. One of the daughters helped her to dry her clothes. They brought her food and drink. Slowly, she began to revive from her ordeal. Ann and Kian were put to bed, after being fed.

"Ma'm, you can't go on today. The river's too high to cross," said Mr. Alexander. "You can wait with us until it goes down a little."

11

"But I can't wait," Jane answered. "My husband is waiting for me. I have to go on." She refused all their arguments. She was deaf to their pleas.

The next morning they mounted their mules. They swam them across the fast running river. It was ten o'clock before they were actually on their way. The mud and slush did not slow Jane down. She kept on hurrying the group. At sundown Jane's efforts were rewarded. They could see the old mission at Nacogdoches.

In only a matter of minutes she was in the arms of her beloved James. The hard struggle was over. She was back where she belonged.

"James, I'll never let you leave me again," she told her husband. In her mind she pictured the old happy life on the plantation with her family.

General Long held his trembling wife. He tried to comfort her. But he knew that this would be only a short reunion. He was already making plans to leave for Galveston. However, he would leave Jane, Ann, and Kian in comfort. They had a room in the old stone fort. That was enough for Jane. But as the wife of the general, she would have the best quarters. She felt that this was a haven for her family.

"We can be comfortable here," she told James. "Don't worry about us. I can make it just as pleasant as our home in Natchez."

He held her a long time in his arms before he began to tell her of his plans.

"Jane, I hate to tell you this, but I must go to Galveston. You have heard of the pirate, Jean Lafitte? He has a fort there. I feel sure that I can get his help," James began in a soft voice. "I must have his aid in my plans. I have waited here for you. Now I must be off to Galveston."

General Long postponed his trip to Galveston

for only a few more days. Before he could leave, an unhappy message came for the Longs. The baby, Rebecca, left with the Calvits in Alexandria, had died. Jane blamed herself for leaving her baby. She wept in great agony. James did his best to comfort her.

"I could have brought her with me," Jane cried. "I shouldn't have left our little one so soon. It's my fault that our Rebecca is dead!"

James held her to his breast. He patted her as one would pat a baby. "Don't cry, dearest. You are not to blame. It wasn't your fault that she didn't live. We still have our Ann, and there'll be other children."

Jane rested in his arms, sobbing in great gasps.

The next morning General Long began making his plans to go to Galveston. He gave strict instructions to Captain Cook, who was to be in charge of the fort. But General Long did not realize the type of officers he had left to care for Jane. Cook proceeded to drink. He became so drunk that he lost control of the others. Things went from bad to worse. There was no discipline at the fort.

Jane tried to send word to her husband. But before she could reach him, news came that put the camp into panic. Colonel Perez was on his way to Nacogdoches with a large force. Perez intended to drive Long out of Texas. Jane was in a state of fear. She knew that the soldiers could not hold off the huge Spanish forces.

Jane started another message to her husband. She told him that she was leaving for Brown's place. General Long was about thirty miles above Galveston when he learned that Perez' forces were right behind him. He sent messages to his forces to make a stand at Nacogdoches. If they failed there, they were to meet him at Bolivar.

The failure with Lafitte had left him depressed. He had tried to show the pirate the value of the republic. Lafitte was not interested. The pirates' base at Campeache was Lafitte's only interest.

General Long hurried on toward Nacogdoches. He went by the Brown farm to see about Jane. She tried to tell him that all was lost at the fort. But he insisted upon going to Nacogdoches. He promised Jane that he would return soon. Then he headed toward the fort.

About this time news spread that the Indians were attacking the settlers. Jane agreed to leave with the Browns for the Sabine. When General Long returned from Nacogdoches, he found that his family had gone on to Louisiana. He finally caught up with them. He sent Jane, Ann, and Kian on to Alexandria.

"Jane, you must return to your sister's home right now. We must have more money to continue this work," James Long told his saddened wife. "I know it's hard. You have lost all your belongings. But we'll get everything back. Just give me a little time to satisfy the people who lent us the money." Again he held his sobbing wife.

II

Point Bolivar

James Long sighed. His loss could not even be measured. It seemed his dream would never come true.

"Jane, I don't know whether it's worth all the cost, this fight to take Texas," James told his wife. He was thinking about the death of his younger brother, David Long. David had been surprised and killed by Indians during the first filibuster.

"But, James, just think of all the men who believe in what you're doing," answered his wife. She was always loyal to her dear James. Dozens of Long's men were eager to go on with the fight. They were ready to go back to Texas under his command.

"I know, Jane, but for this I must have more money. I just don't know where it's coming from," James said. In New Orleans he might raise some funds, but he did not even have the money to go there. He had friends in the city who were interested in his plans. But how to get there, he did not know.

Finally, James Long set out in an open canoe, a pirogue that was nothing more than a hollowed-out log. The trip was uncomfortable, as he told Jane later.

"But comfort was not important," said the unhappy James. "I failed to get anyone to put up the money for our efforts. I don't know where to turn next. I just knew that Colonel Ramsey would be able to help me."

"What about the trading post at Natchitoches?" said Jane. "Won't that give us some of the money that we need?"

"I'm sorry, Jane. I came back by Natchitoches. You won't believe what happened there. Jim Smith tried to waylay me. He shot at me just outside the trading post. There was no money there. Instead Smith had actually made debts for me. I can't tell you how much that man has done to us!" James told her. He felt that all was lost. He would never be able to make Texas a part of the United States!

Sadly, they returned to their home in Natchez. But there was a surprise waiting for them. Once more, there were people who believed in James Long and his cause. They were willing to aid him at present. They were even willing to promise future funds. His friends in Natchez and Alexandria would see that he had a second chance!

Again James Long began making plans for another trip to Texas.

"Jane, I tell you, I will go to Point Bolivar. I will establish a fort. Once more we will be on our way!" James shouted excitedly to his wife.

"I know you will succeed, James," said Jane. She was very confident that her husband could do what he promised.

"I will ask Warren D. C. Hall to go with me to Texas. Together we can put together the forces we need to defeat the Spanish," James said. He felt certain that things were finally going right.

It didn't take Jane Long very much time to decide that she would go with her husband to Texas. After all, she had decided that she would never be parted from him again.

"Jane, I know that you want to go," said James, "but surely you know the dangers that we'll face. We just can't take little Ann into all of that."

"James, her future is our future. We must try to make a life for us, wherever you are," pleaded Jane. She felt that having James leave her again would break her heart.

James answered her slowly, "I know how you feel, Jane. Perhaps you can make up your mind if you go alone with me. If you decide that it is not right for Ann, then I can send you back with an escort." He thought that perhaps a taste of Texas would satisfy Jane. She loved Ann very much. He knew that she would want only the best of life for Ann.

They left Ann with the Calvits in Alexandria. There they hired a small sailing vessel. They loaded the boat with the supplies for their trip. It was early springtime when they left Calcasieu, Louisiana, for their new Texas adventure. The weather was good. It was a pleasant trip.

When they arrived at Point Bolivar, the flowers were in bloom. The countryside was lovely. One could not ask for more. There was plenty of wild game. Oysters and fish were there for the taking. Jane fell in love with the place. Point Bolivar would be her real home!

"James, this is delightful. We'll live right here for the rest of our lives. Isn't it wonderful?" Jane said.

"Listen to me, Jane. This is no place for a home right now. Later, perhaps it will be," James tried to reason with her. He knew that life would be hard. Texas was not yet safe for a woman. He feared for her safety and that of young Ann.

"But, James, you know that my home is wherever you are," cried Jane.

James wisely said nothing more. He hoped that a few weeks would change Jane's mind. It was lonely here. A child needed other children to play with. Surely Jane would realize that fact, sooner or later. Just give her a little more time.

A stronghold was set up at Bolivar. Long's small force of 130 men established a crude mud fort. They mounted the single cannon. That would have to serve as their defense.

The men and their families lived in tents beside the fort. There were signs of life across the bay. Campeache, as Jean Lafitte called his settlement of pirates, was alive with movement.

"James, look! There's a fire. Campeache is on fire!" Jane shouted. They watched as the entire settlement was being lighted by torch, one house after another. No one seemed to be trying to put out the fire. Instead, they were trying to spread the fire.

"What can they be about?" James said. "Is the man mad? Something is certainly wrong over there." James climbed to the top of the fort in order to have a clearer view of the island.

Suddenly, they saw a boat putting out from the island. The men rowed swiftly toward Point Bolivar. James shaded his eyes to get a better view of the boat. There were four men in it.

James' curiosity was excited by the strange activity. Why was Campeache in ruins? Had there been a riot or a mutiny? He thought of protecting his own settlement. But four men could not harm his larger group of men. He watched in silence as the boat put in to shore. One of the men waded out upon the beach. As he reached the little group gathered on the beach, he held out a letter. James Long stepped forward to take the letter. He ripped open the seal. Silently, he read the letter. Then he smiled broadly.

"Jane, it is an invitation," Long told his wife. "He wants us to have dinner with him aboard his ship, the *Pride*."

James turned to his wife and waited for her reply. He was amused now, but full of questions.

"He is being polite, James, but ask the man about the fires," answered Jane. She was the practical one of the two. What on earth could cause a man to burn his own home, and then issue an invitation to dinner? The man must be crazy, demented, wild. Thoughts ran through her mind.

But while she was thinking, James was asking questions. The man listened to James. But each time he simply shook his head and said, "No sabe, señor."

"There is no way to get this man to talk. All he will say is 'I don't know.' He doesn't want to talk," James told the group waiting with him. James understood Spanish well enough, but the man just wouldn't answer. He didn't know. That was the only reason he would give.

"Well, Jane, I don't have time to fool with this. I'll just refuse the invitation. I'm not going to waste my time on board that vessel," Long told his wife.

"But, James, I want to go. I've never seen him. I'm curious about the man. Please, James, I want to go," Jane begged.

"Do you really want to visit that pirate?" he asked. He was not surprised at his wife's reaction. He knew her keen disappointment if he refused the invitation.

"Oh, James, imagine! Dinner with a pirate on board his ship!" Jane was excited.

"Well, it will be a rare experience for you, Jane," James told his wife kindly. "Perhaps you can learn something of his plans. I would really like to know what this fire is all about."

Jane was already planning the trip across the bay. She had heard that Lafitte was a gallant gentleman. In fact, all kinds of romantic tales had been told about him in Louisiana. She would wear her best dress. Her hair was fresh washed in rainwater. She would be as pretty as any woman he had ever entertained.

James Long sent the messenger back to Lafitte, accepting the invitation for Jane. He would send Ben Milam as her escort. Kian could go along with her.

"Jane, do find out what you can about his plans," James told his wife. "I must know what all this business is about."

"I'll do what I can, anyway," promised Jane. "I can always talk people into things, James. Surely, I can manage this pirate."

The appointed time for the visit arrived. Jane had been ready and waiting for quite some time. James sent four of his men to row the party over to the waiting vessel. He walked down to the beach with Jane. There he carried her out to the boat. Gently, he kissed her after he had placed her on the front seat.

"Have a good time, Jane," he told her. "Remember, I will be waiting to hear your report."

"James, isn't this exciting? I can hardly wait to see him," Jane answered.

All eyes were turned toward the *Pride*, floating proudly out in the bay. This would be a visit that Jane would long remember. James had carried Kian out, also. The young Negro maid was almost as excited as Jane. Her dark eyes shone brightly.

"Missy Jane," Kian cried, "Missy Jane, we is going to have us a fine time."

Ben Milam took his seat behind Jane and Kian.

"I'll take good care of them, James," he told the smiling James Long.

"I know you will, Ben. Otherwise I would not let them go," answered James.

If Jane Long had expected to find the pirate chief a rough, crude giant, she was disappointed. All the reports about Jean Lafitte were confusing. Gossip about him was widespread. She had heard many stories about his terrible temper. Instead, Jane was pleasingly disappointed. He was the very opposite of what she had imagined him to be.

The pirate chief came to offer his hand as she stepped on board the *Pride*. He was handsome, graceful, and polite. He was not a giant, as she had pictured him. Instead, he was of medium height. His hair was dark, and he had a pair of vivid, sparkling dark eyes. His soft, gentle speech pleased Jane.

"Madame, I welcome you to my ship. It is to be regretted that your husband could not come with you," Jean Lafitte told Jane. He bowed low over her hand.

Jane was escorted to a salon, where a lavish meal was set. The china was fine and shining. The crystal was thin and sparkling. Gold service plates were laid before each guest. The centerpiece was of delicious tropical fruits.

Jane gazed around the table, fascinated with the service. Kian stood behind Jane's chair, ready to help her mistress if she should be needed. The faithful Kian was very watchful of Jane.

The talk was sparkling, full of witty remarks, stories of exciting and thrilling adventures, and compliments for the beautiful Mrs. Long. Jane did her best to obtain some news from her host. Lafitte politely avoided any of her attempts. He managed the conversation. Jane came away from the meeting with very little knowledge of the pirate's plans. His future base was still his secret.

At the end of the delightful evening, Jane told

her host good-bye and returned to the long boat.

"James, I'm sorry," she told her waiting husband. "I just couldn't get him to say anything about where he intends to go. I tried everything I could, but it just wouldn't work."

"I was afraid of that, Jane. I could have told you that he is a very private person. He just doesn't talk about his business," said James. He knew that if anyone could have persuaded Lafitte to talk, it would be Jane. "Oh, well, Jane, don't worry. He just isn't interested. He's had his taste of life on land. I'm sure that he'll never come back to Galveston. He was born to live and die on the sea."

"But, James, I did have a wonderful time. You should have seen the meal that we had. The service was perfect," said Jane happily.

Jane's first visit to Bolivar was brief. General Long ordered the men who planned to remain with him to report there by April 10, 1820. He put Walker in charge. Then Jane, Warren D. C. Hall, and General Long left for Alexandria. They wasted no time in going after their daughter Ann. From Alexandria they moved on to New Orleans.

There Jane had several weeks to think about the Texas venture. She had some doubts about taking little Ann back into that wild land. It might not be right for Ann.

"I'm not sure that we should take Ann back with us. She is so tiny," said Jane. "I'm afraid she'll become ill. We just can't lose another child to the wilderness."

"I'm sure you are right, Jane," answered her husband. He knew the terrible trial that it might be for both Jane and the child. He wanted Jane with him all the time, but the life would be so difficult for her. However, it was Jane's choice to make. He already knew that he could not tell Jane what to do. She was such a brave, fearless young woman!

"I will leave Ann with my sister in Rodney, Mississippi. She will be all right there. We can get things in better order at Point Bolivar. Perhaps we can even build a good cabin at the fort!" cried Jane. Having made up her mind, at once she began to plan for the future. She could hardly wait to get back to that beautiful place which she had chosen for her home.

That very evening James came back to their rooms full of his own plans.

"Jane, I have my money finally. A group of Americans are going to pay for our entire expedition. That's not all. They have promised future aid for our colony," shouted the happy James Long. He swung Jane around in his arms and kissed her soundly. Little Ann danced around the two of them, sensing her parents' happiness.

"There is one problem," added James Long. "They want the expedition to be led by someone who will have the loyalty of the Mexican leaders. They have chosen José Felix Trespalacios. I'm not sure that I like it, but I can get along with him. This is such a good chance to carry out our plan for Texas."

"James, after all, freeing Texas from the Spanish is the first step. The question of making Texas a part of the United States can be solved later," Jane said. "We can just wait for time to take care of the problem."

The question of money was solved. The next step was to prepare for the trip back to Bolivar. Jane left for Rodney with Ann. While she was gone, James secured provisions for the trip. He bought the necessary arms and ammunition. He hired boats to carry the party to Texas. He secured all the materials that were necessary for the expedition.

However, Jane did not get back as soon as expected. The two boats were loaded, but they waited several days for Jane to return. James Long was waiting impatiently when she finally rode up to the docks.

"I'm sorry, James," she said. "It was just that I hated to leave my baby."

James answered her kindly, "Don't worry, Jane. We were busy while we were waiting. Everything is ready. You will sail on the *Three Sisters* with Ben Milam and John Austin. I will go on the sloop with the arms and ammunition."

"But, James, I wanted to sail with you," Jane protested. "I don't want us to be apart so long."

"Jane, you know that we have to take the munitions out without letting the officials know," James told her. "They would never let us leave if they found out about our plans. I will slip out through the bayous. The *Three Sisters* can sail right down the Mississippi since all you have on board is food and supplies."

"Of course, James, I wasn't really thinking. I know that you must be careful," answered Jane.

Long's sloop slipped up the river and cut through Vermilion Bay. He was on his way to Texas. But the *Three Sisters* was not so lucky. Just as they were about to weigh anchor, the ship was boarded by a customs officer. He was looking for contraband articles of war. James had already gone. There was nothing for the officer to do. He would have to let them leave.

Then the officer surprised the passengers and crew. He asked to see Mrs. Long's trunks.

"Indeed, you will not go through my trunks. I have packed everything very carefully. I will not allow such a search!" Jane said angrily.

"But, Madame, I represent the United States government. We have the right to search any ship that leaves these shores," said the customs man.

"You will not open my trunks," argued Jane. "If you insist upon such, I will have my trunks taken ashore right this minute.

She called for some of the crew to remove her belongings. Jane had no intention of letting this man bully her. Just as the bosun and his men were picking up the trunks, the custom man returned.

"Madame Long, I must apologize. It was not my intention to upset you unduly. I was only doing my duty. I am sure that you are not hiding such illegal goods. My apology, Madame," the customs agent said. He was still not sure of Mrs. Long. After all, her husband had already carried out one invasion of Texas. Another such venture might bring down the fury of Spain upon the United States. Governments had to be careful of such actions.

At last the vessel got underway. They were already late for the meeting at Point Bolivar. But the ship had only reached English Bend, the first turn in the Mississippi, when Jane decided that she could not leave little Ann. Jane went to the captain to explain that she had to go back for Ann.

When they met an English ship, the *Three Sisters* was heaved to. Jane went aboard the ship and returned to her sister's home in Rodney. There she picked up Ann and carried her back to the waiting *Three Sisters*. The captain breathed a sigh of relief as the vessel once again hoisted sail.

Jane Long finally arrived at Point Bolivar to make her home. In spite of the delay, they got there about the same time as James Long's ship. James held her in his arms, kissing her tenderly.

"Jane, I am so glad to have you back. And I'm very happy that you decided to bring our baby girl.

We can make Ann safe and happy here with us," he promised.

"James, I brought everything we need. I have Ann and Kian, and there are many of our personal things to make this seem like home," Jane answered happily. "We'll make this our real home now."

Soon General Long's quarters were cheerful and homelike. There were other women at the post. Two doctors' wives kept Jane company. They busied themselves with their homemaking duties. The men worked on the fortress and cleared the land for cabins, which they would build later.

Often they gazed across the bay, wondering about Jean Lafitte and his burned-out settlement. Sometimes they could see activity there.

"It's only the Indians who used to live there," James told Jane. "I don't think they will bother us. After all, we have the fort. They can't hurt us here."

"But, James, aren't they Karankawas? We've heard the terrible stories about the bad things they do to people who fall into their hands," Jane answered. She knew that they were reputed to be cannibals. What a terrible thing to be! Jane's imagination did frightening things to her mind.

The Karankawas were a tall, powerful race of men. They had inhabited this coast since before the white man came to these shores. Lafitte's pirates had dealt them much misery, driving them away from their island. Their hatred of the white man had grown during Lafitte's time.

The settlers on Point Bolivar often gazed at the island, both curiosity and fear filling their hearts. Then came the horrible day when they heard the screams of a ship load of French settlers. The Indians had boarded the ship during the night. Now they were hauling their captives to the shore.

"General Long, they're killing them," cried one of Long's men.

"Get the long boats ready," commanded Long. "We will have to try to rescue them." The men hurried to carry out the command. But before they could push off from shore, it was clear that they could never make it in time. The Indians greatly outnumbered General Long's forces. It would be foolish to attack. The settlers stood in silence, filled with pity for those other helpless beings. For days they could not look across the bay at the island. It would be a long time before the horror of the act left them.

During these days at Point Bolivar, James Long was not forgetting his plans for Texas. However, his hands were filled with problems. Trespalacios had arrived at Bolivar. General Long did not like the man, but he tried to accept him. The man caused problems with some of the men. He insisted that they work. The men were resentful of his authority. There was even one time when James Long had to go to New Orleans to rescue Trespalacios from some trouble.

Later a woman named Mary Crow caused trouble among the men. General Long had to reprimand her. Modello, Trespalacios' secretary, defended Mary Crow. He spoke with disrespect to General Long. Long had the secretary arrested. The man resisted arrest and was shot by a guard. This action caused an unpleasant feeling between Long and Trespalacios.

General Long had sent his runners to the Spanish-held settlements of La Bahía and Bexar. Reports were coming back about the plans of the Mexican revolutionists. Agustín de Iturbide and Santa Anna were planning to carry out a plot

27

against Spain to free Texas. General Long decided that Trespalacios and Ben Milam should leave at once for Vera Cruz to meet with Iturbide. They were hardly on their way when the news came that Bexar and La Bahía had declared their independence.

"Jane, this is it! I must sail for Copano Bay at once. With this news, I am sure that we can win. We cannot lose any time in getting our forces together," James told his wife.

Jane Long answered her husband, "Dear James, take care of yourself. Hurry back to us."

Jane's life had been made up of meeting and parting with her husband. This was no different from any other time.

"Jane, I'll be gone only about three weeks, and when I return, I'm sure that I'll have some wonderful news for all of our friends," James told her. "Stay here until I return. If I can't get back here, I'll send a message about where to meet me. Stay in our home. I'll be back with you soon."

With his words echoing in her mind, Jane watched the general and his men sail away. This was the last time that Jane Long saw her beloved husband. Little did she know that he would never return to her.

III

The Tragic Winter

The little colony at Point Bolivar was filled with happiness. The days were spent in working in the family gardens. Life was very easy for them.

"Ann, Ann," called Jane Long. "I need you to help with the watering." Jane was busy carrying fresh water from the well. She watered her tiny carrots, turnips, potatoes, and onions. The fall weather was perfect for growing these winter garden plants. With luck like this, there would be plenty of food for the cold weather. Some of the men had dug a cave for her. She would store the vegetables there for the winter. The onions would be perfect in a good stew. Jane could make a delicious supper with a little venison.

"Mama!" cried Ann, "I can't come. I am busy. There is a great big old crab nibbling at my line. I can get him in and we'll have crab gumbo tonight!" Ann was delighted with her new job. She was busy helping the family.

Jane smiled as she watched her small daughter bending over the little pond. Ann enjoyed getting some of the food for their evening meal. These first days were happy ones for Jane Long and her little family.

Jane had a very happy smile now. She knew that there was to be another child in the Long fam-

29

ily. Soon she would be ready to tell Kian and Ann about the coming child.

James Long would be home long before the baby was due. Then Jane would be perfectly happy. She was young and beautiful. The others at the fort admired and respected this young wife of their leader.

"Mrs. Long, there are some men who want to work on the roof of your tent," said the lady who was standing outside the fort. "They think that it must be stronger when the winter winds blow."

"Of course, they can," Jane answered. "I am glad that they are taking care of it. I knew that it was not too strong. James said before he left that it should be worked on."

"You know, Mrs. Long," said Mrs. Allen, "we may have a hard winter. I do hope that the men will get back soon. We need more supplies before the bad weather sets in."

"They will be back soon," Jane told her. "We will have plenty of food for the winter. The garden will grow as I know it will. We'll have fresh vegetables until cold weather. I even have a few tomato plants that have some fruit on them. I'll store the green ones to ripen for the winter."

"But, surely, Mrs. Long, you don't eat the horrible things! They're poison. My grandmother said that they sometimes put them on the mantle. It gives the fireplace a bright color. But the seeds will kill you if you eat them!" cried Mrs. Allen. She was terrified at the thought of swallowing the seeds.

"Mrs. Allen, of course we'll eat them," Jane said. "They make wonderful stews, and gumbo wouldn't be the same without them."

Mrs. Allen just shook her head as she walked back to her tent. There was really no way of reasoning with Mrs. Long. This Jane Long had a mind of her own. Tomatoes!! Imagine what Grandmother Allen would say to crab gumbo! Oh, well.

Then as the days went by, no word came from James Long. He had said about three weeks. A month had passed, and no word from him. The soldiers began to desert the fort. They had decided among themselves that Long wasn't coming back.

"But, sir, you can't just go off and leave us here!" Jane Long told one of the men as he hurried to pack his pirogue.

"Ma'm, I'm sorry, but I can trade with the Indians. Perhaps I will hear something from them about General Long," the man answered.

Jane tried to talk the man out of his plan to leave, but she couldn't. He was not the only one. Others began to talk of going to New Orleans. They were even bold enough to say that there might be a better way to take Texas from the Spanish.

"But, listen," Jane pleaded with one group who was planning to leave, "You know that General Long is depending upon you to be here when he needs you."

"Ma'm, we can't wait here forever. He was supposed to be back long before this time," they answered her. How could she argue with them? There was no way of knowing when James Long would return. What had become of him? Jane Long was filled with horrible thoughts of what might have happened to him. But then her better judgment set in. She knew that James Long would return to her and Ann!

One morning Dr. and Mrs. Edgar came to talk with Jane. They had decided that they could not stay any longer. The food was running out. They knew that the end was coming. Mrs. Edgar begged Jane to go with them to New Orleans.

31

"Jane, dear, you must go with us," Mrs. Edgar said. "After all, we can't leave you alone here in this wild place. You have only a child and a slave to protect you. You need to be with some of your family when this new baby arrives! "

"I know you mean well, Mrs. Edgar," answered Jane. "But I can't leave. James expects me to be waiting for him. He will be back before long."

"Jane, you know that he will find you wherever you go," Mrs. Edgar told her. Dr. Edgar urged her to think of the safety of the new baby. She couldn't stay here with just Kian to help her.

"James left me here to stay until he returns. I will do what he said," Jane said. "If I die, he will find my bones. I can't leave until he comes for me."

The soldiers continued to desert. They took supplies with them. One even took the steel mill and the last barrel of flour. Finally, the doctor and the two women knew that they must also leave. Again they begged Jane to go with them.

"We will take you to Alexandria or Natchez, wherever you want to go," Dr. Edgar said.

"My husband left me here, and I must stay until he returns," Jane answered. "Otherwise he would never know where to find me." She refused to admit that anything could have happened to General Long.

Dr. and Mrs. Edgar and Mrs. Allen made ready to leave. They bid Jane a tearful good-bye.

"Jane, try to take care of yourself. I pray to God that General Long will return soon," said Mrs. Allen.

"We'll manage all right. Don't worry about us," Jane told her. "Kian is good at fishing. Ann catches crab every day. We will have everything we need. Don't worry."

After they had sailed away, Jane checked her supplies. There was very little to check. The mackerel barrels were almost empty. The salty liquid remained in the barrels. She made a mental note that fish could be kept in salt water. They would have to work hard to build up their food supplies.

Jane found plenty of ammunition, a few muskets, several fishhooks, and one line for fishing. They would certainly have to take good care of that one line. Ann could go crabbing with only a few strings of cloth. But to catch the big fish they would have to use the one line.

"Kian, we must keep the garden alive as long as we can. I just hope a freeze doesn't come before the last turnips are dug," Jane told the girl. Thus by hunting and fishing, Jane managed to keep her little family alive.

Now they were all alone except for the dog "Galveston." Jane had the devoted Kian to keep her and Ann company. Kian would have died for Jane at any time if necessary. Jane knew how much Kian thought of her and Ann.

"Ma'm, Miss Jane, you know that we can make it! General Long will be back. We knows he's comin' back. Don't ever forget that! " said Kian. "He'll be proud of you, Ma'm."

Kian was washing their few clothes in water from the little stream. There was no soap, but Kian knew how to soak them in a solution of ashes and water. That would make them fresher. Kian knew how to do so many things. Jane watched her at the chore. She mentally thanked God for the good servant, Kian. She didn't know how she could ever have managed without Kian's help.

Jane watched the island across the bay. Galveston Island seemed to be a long way off.

However, Jane knew that the day would come when the evil Karankawas would see her campfires. They would be certain to come to Point Bolivar. She feared that day that would bring them to the shores of the Point. She watched the shoreline every day. Sometimes she could see them rowing their canoes out in the bay. They would be certain to come.

Then one day Jane remembered a story that she had heard in her childhood. It would keep Ann and Kian from getting bored in their line life. Besides that, she needed to know when the Indians started toward Bolivar.

"Ann, Kian, come here. I have a story to tell you," Jane shouted. Both of them came running. Kian loved a good story as much as little Ann did.

"Once upon a time, there was a man who was shipwrecked upon a deserted island," began Jane.

"Like us, Mama? Like us?" Ann cried.

"Yes, Ann, very much like us. No one came to the island. Robinson Crusoe, as they called him, had to fish and hunt for his food, just as we do," answered Jane to her eagerly waiting audience.

"Mis' Jane, didn't he have nobody with him?" asked Kian.

"No, Kian, he was all alone. He managed to fish and got along fine for a long time. But then one day he was walking along the shore. Suddenly he saw footsteps on the beach," Jane continued.

Ann and Kian listened excitedly. Already their eager minds were picturing footsteps on their beach. Jane finished the story of Robinson Crusoe and Friday. But she had hardly said the last word when both Kian and Ann dashed out toward the beach. They walked along eagerly looking for the possible footsteps. In fact, they spent hours in this interesting game. Every morning with Kian right behind her, Ann ran out to check the beach.

Then came the day when Kian came running back, shouting to Jane. "Mis' Jane, Mis' Jane, there's steps on the beach. I found 'em right down by the edge of the water," Kian cried.

"Mama, Mama, the Indians have been here," Ann yelled, as she ran toward the fort.

Jane knew that the Indians had been sneaking around to see who was in the fort. She wondered how much they knew about the little group that lived in it! She tried to remain calm in front of Ann and Kian. They were so scared that she had to quiet their fears some way.

"Ann, get my red petticoat from the tent. We'll hang it on the flag pole. The Indians will think it is a flag," Jane told her daughter. She hoped the sight of the red flag would frighten any who came near the Point.

That night Jane, Ann, and Kian sat outside watching the campfires of the Indians across the bay on Galveston Island. There was no way of knowing what day or what hour they might decide to attack the fort. They would certainly murder the three.

Several times they saw the Indians go down to the beach. It seemed they were about to get into their canoes. However, the flag must have scared them off. They did not attack.

Jane loaded and primed the little brass cannon. She carefully covered it with an oiled canvas. This way it would be safe from the salt water. But it would be ready if they should need it. They set watches. Thus they could be ready if the Indians started across the bay. Ann and Kian took the daytime watches. Jane sat near the cannon at night. She hoped that cold weather would set in soon. She knew that the Indians would go back to the mainland then.

Not too many mornings later Ann saw the Indians swarming out into their canoes. She shouted to Jane and Kian that they were coming.

"Ann, Kian, get inside the fort," commanded Jane. Then she took her position by the cannon. She had the lighted towrope in hand for the match. She watched the canoes coming toward the Point. James had told her to wait until the enemy was close enough. Jane tried to think of all the things he had told her about the cannon. Waiting was hard to do. It seemed forever that she waited. Then luck was with her. She touched the fire to the powder. Her aim was sure. The solid shot fell among the first canoes.

Furiously Jane sponged the heated barrel. She reloaded and primed the cannon. She was ready for a second shot at the canoes. But it wasn't needed. The war canoes turned and headed back toward the island. Jane watched, her hands shaking. Her whole body felt numb from the fright. It was hard to believe that she had really done it. The Indians were driven back this time.

Jane looked down. Both Kian and Ann were standing beside her. She wondered how long they had been beside her. She sat down beside the cannon. She put her arms around Ann. Kian was beside herself with excitement.

"Mis' Jane, you done it! You drove them Indians away," cried Kian. The look she gave Jane was one of complete worship. Kian knew now that Jane could do anything.

"Mama, Mama, will they come back?" Ann asked.

"Ann, I don't know. We were lucky this time. Perhaps this will be enough for them. Maybe they won't come back, but we'll have to be ready for them anyway," answered Jane.

The Indians did come back. This time, Jane was ready for them. They got the same treatment that they had received the first time. The war canoes hurriedly turned back toward the shores of Galveston Island. This was the last time that they tried to attack the fort.

It was not long before winter set in with a real fury. Wind whipped the water into icy foam. The chilling wind froze the poor women to the bone.

"Mis' Jane, I don't think I'se ever been this cold afore," Kian complained. Her clothes were becoming threadbare. She suffered from the cold more than did Jane or Ann.

Jane answered her kindly, "Kian, perhaps it won't be too long. James will come after us. Then we can get some warmer clothes."

"Mama, I hope he comes soon. I don't like this place now," Ann said. The bad weather kept Ann from playing on the beach. She missed the fishing and hunting for footsteps.

The water in the bay began to freeze over. Gradually, the animals had begun to go out upon the ice. Jane watched bear and other animals cross from the mainland to Galveston Island.

One morning she heard Kian shouting to her. Jane ran to the beach to see what Kian wanted.

"Mis' Jane, there's some ducks frozen in the water. Their feet's caught in the ice," Kian told her.

"That's our supper tonight, Kian," Jane said. "We'll chop them out of the ice. They'll make a fine roast. Just think, Kian, we'll have roast duckling. Won't that be a real treat?"

Busily, they worked at chopping the ducks out of the ice. Kian started heating water to dress the ducks. Ann danced around the fire, shouting first to Kian and then to Jane.

"We're going to have a fine dinner tonight," said Ann. "I'm going to set the table. It'll be just like a party!"

Jane told her little family, "At least, the ice is good for one thing. We can keep the ducks for awhile. The ice will keep them fresh."

The supply of ducks lasted for a week or so. Then the little group began to run out of food again. Their dry provisions had run out long before. Finally, they were down to salted fish. Luckily, they could dig the frozen fish out of the frozen bay. Dozens of them were caught in the ice.

Jane and Kian broke the ice with hatchets. They dug them out. Then they carefully packed them in the brine of the mackerel barrels. At last they had a good supply of fish put away. They could live through the bad spell that was just starting.

Jane took time to inspect the clothing that had been left at the fort. She and Kian had already started wearing the leftover men's clothing. Most of the coats and shirts were too big for Ann, but Jane started cutting them down to fit. Their own clothing had become too ragged to wear.

One morning Jane was awakened by Kian. She could hardly stand up beside her bed. The ice had pushed the tent down so far that it was almost touching the bed.

"Mis' Jane, it's gonna break. Then we'll be covered with ice, too," Kian said.

"I know, Kian," answered Jane. "I just don't know what we can do about it. We can just pray that it doesn't break. I know the men put the best canvas we had left over it." She eyed the sagging tent sadly. It seemed their troubles would never end. But there was always the hope that James Long would hurry back to them. Where could he be? She knew that he would not desert them here. Then, too, there was the baby that he did not even know about. Jane prayed that he would get back before the new baby arrived.

One morning Jane and Kian were gathering food for their fire. Ann screamed and pointed in the direction of the mainland.

"Mama, there's a bear out on the water!" Ann shouted.

Jane looked up and saw a huge black bear moving awkwardly across the thick ice of the bay.

"Kian, get my gun," Jane shouted to Kian.

About that time the dog Galveston saw the bear. He began barking loudly. The noise must have scared the bear. He began loping back toward the west.

Snow drifted into the rude tent. The winds nearly blew the roof off. The short supply of firewood would hardly keep them warm. Their days were spent in leaning over the small fire or hunting for pieces of wood that they could burn.

One night Jane found Kian desperately ill. The second day of her illness, Jane knew that Kian had pneumonia. She kept the tent as warm as she could. She nursed the sick Kian night and day. Ann tried her best to help. She dragged in all the dead branches that she could find. Jane and Ann hunted for food while Kian lay tossing about with a high fever.

On the night of December 21, 1821, there was a cold wind howling about the fort. Kian was so ill that she was delirious. Alone, Jane Long gave birth to her third child, a tiny and frail little girl. Jane named her Mary James Long. The next morning Jane was up and hunting food for her family. One mercy was granted to Jane. The faithful Kian did not die.

When Kian was able to walk, she and Jane took an old hammock and made a fish net. They went to the bayou and caught three small mullets.

"These little fish will make good bait. We'll catch us a big flounder or a redfish with these. A good red snapper will taste real fine, won't it?" asked Kian.

"Kian, let's just hope we catch something. I know that you and Ann are as hungry as I am," Jane answered.

Jane put a hook on their last line. She carefully baited the hook with one of the mullet that they had caught.

"Mis' Jane, don't go too far out in the surf," Kian said. "Be careful you don't fall down."

Jane felt a slight tug on the line. She wrapped the end of the line around her waist and tied it together. Then she walked a few steps further out into the water. Suddenly, there came a great tug on the line. Jane tried to untie the line.

"Mis' Jane, be careful," called Kian.

"Kian, I can't untie it. It's pulling me further out!" Jane yelled. She worked feverishly at the line.

"Cut the line. Please cut it, Mis' Jane!" Kian shouted. Jane took her knife and sawed at the line. It finally separated. The fish surfaced as the line gave away. Jane and Kian saw a big red fish swimming out in the bay. It was pulling their only line with it.

"Well, Kian, now we'll just have to eat oysters and crabs. That's all we'll have now. I'm sorry I lost the line," said Jane. There were tears in her eyes as she stared at the surface of the water. There she had seen the redfish swim away. Sometimes life seemed so hard.

Christmas was coming soon. It wouldn't be like the others they had known. However, there was one problem that was solved. Ann had replaced her old rag doll with little Mary James. She lovingly took care of her little sister. Ann wouldn't expect a new doll for Christmas. Not with her new baby sister, Mary James. She took great joy in caring for the baby. While Kian and Jane hunted for food, Ann stayed by Mary James' cradle.

When Mary James was five days old, joyful news was brought to Jane. Kian came running in from the beach. There were seven men in a boat. Full of excitement, Kian, Ann, and Jane watched as the boat was beached.

"Ma'm, are you Mrs. Long?" asked the group's leader.

"I am Mrs. Long," answered Jane. "Do you have any word from my husband? He is General Long. Have you heard anything about him? Where is he?"

"I am Captain Rafael Gonzales. I have brought you a letter from your husband," said the captain. "He is in Monterrey."

Jane eagerly tore the letter open. It was James Long's handwriting! Swiftly she read the letter. It told her that he would be home soon. He had gone on to Monterrey because he was not successful in Bahía.

"Kian, he's coming home soon," she shouted to the waiting Kian and Ann. "He will be home before long. It's all over now. We won't suffer any more. James is coming home!"

The men stayed for two days. They hunted for a deer or an antelope to feed the starving women. After butchering the deer they had killed, they prepared to leave. At least, they were leaving plenty of food for the women. They disliked leaving the women alone. However, they had their own mission to carry out. After all, General Long would arrive

41

before long. Of that fact they were sure.

Jane waited patiently. She was also sure that her husband would arrive soon. The New Year of 1822 came in. There was no sound other than the lapping of the waves upon the shore. The long days went by, one by one, but no news came of James Long. A long, lonely time passed. Not a soul came near the Point. Finally, there came a time when there was no food for three days.

Kian was down on the beach gathering driftwood for the fire. Suddenly, she looked up and screamed. She rushed in toward the fort.

"Mis' Jane, there's some men coming up the beach. They's not Indians," Kian shouted.

Jane hurriedly put on her shoes. She rushed out to the beach to greet the men. To her great surprise, the men ran away from her.

"Please, wait, please listen to me!" Jane called to them. "I need your help. Please wait for me!"

She ran after them, calling and yelling. They continued to run and were soon out of sight. In deep despair Jane dragged herself back to the fort.

"Kian, they wouldn't stop. Why wouldn't they help us?" Jane said to the disappointed Kian.

"Mis' Jane, maybe they thought we were Indians," Kian answered. Sadly, she began to tie some rags together. She would try to catch a few crabs. It was too cold for them to bite. Still she hoped she might get one or two.

Several days later Ann came running up the beach. She shouted joyously.

"There are some sails out there," she cried. "See, Mama, there they are!"

"They surely are there, Ann," Jane told her happy daughter. She hugged Ann as they both walked further up the beach toward the approaching sails. Kian joined them, clapping her hands excitedly.

The three of them shouted, waved, and ran back and forth on the sand. Their actions must have gotten attention from the fleet of sailboats. Two boats put out toward the shore. Jane and Kian ran down to the water's edge to greet them.

"We're so glad to see you," Jane told the men. "We have been here by ourselves for such a long time."

"I sure hope you brought us some flour," Kian said. "I would really like to have some baked bread."

"I am Mrs. James Long," Jane told them. "Have you heard anything from my husband?"

"Mrs. Long, we have just come from New Orleans, but we do not have any news of your husband," they told the unhappy wife. "But we can help you with some supplies." He called to the men from one of the boats. He ordered them to go back to the vessels for food.

Before long the boat returned with some food, including flour and sugar. Kian could hardly wait to start their supper. Tonight they would have bread for their meal, the first in many months. While Kian was baking the bread, one of the men went into the woods. There he killed a big buck which provided plenty of fresh meat for the hungry women. They would eat well for awhile.

The men were the first of the settlers that were bound for Stephen F. Austin's colony. That night the vessels tied up in Galveston Bay. The next morning they set sail for various points. One went to San Jacinto, up the bay. Another started toward Galveston Island, but was wrecked upon reaching land. Still another vessel sailed for the mouth of the Brazos River.

Jane, Ann, and Kian stood out on the shore, waving toward the last of the vessels. They hated to see them go. There was no way of knowing how long it would be before they would see any more white men.

But they did not have to wait very long. The next day a man appeared, rowing a little pirogue. He kept very close to the shore. Behind him walking along the shore, was his family. He had the pirogue loaded with everything the family owned.

As the man got closer to Jane, she recognized him. He was a Mr. James Smith, whom she had met in Calcasieu, Louisiana.

"Hello, Mrs. Long," he shouted. She waved to him, and then she started walking toward the approaching family.

"Mrs. Smith, it's so good to see another woman!" Jane told her. She shook hands with the woman and then hugged her. Little Ann was beside herself with joy at seeing some other children.

"Jane Long, it's good to find you. We were so worried about you. There have been all kinds of terrible reports," the woman told her.

"You are on your way to a new home?" Jane asked her.

"Indeed, we are," answered Mrs. Smith. "We know that life will be better for us in Texas." She eyed Jane's ragged clothes. Upon seeing her poor condition, she began to beg Jane to go on with her family. They were bound for San Jacinto.

"It will be so much better for you," Mrs. Smith said. "We can help you and look after you and your babies." They had gone into Jane's tent to see little Mary James Long.

But once again Jane Long refused help.

"I can't leave Bolivar. I must wait for my husband here where he left me," she said.

"Well, I will be back before long," Mr. Smith told her. "We'll leave our Peggy here to help you until then." Fifteen-year-old Peggy would keep Jane company. "I will bring you some more supplies from San Jacinto," he continued.

The story of Jane Long's plight spread rapidly among the newcomers to Texas. They all felt sorry for the woman who waited on the lonely shore for her husband. However, life was not so sad for Jane. Colonists were passing up the San Jacinto almost every day. Most of them stopped to talk to Jane. Her question was the same for all of them.

"Have you heard anything from General Long?" she asked. They had all heard rumors about his fate. However, no one could tell her anything for sure.

One of the newcomers was a trader, who sailed along the coast in a little schooner. He came up the river with the settlers. He stopped to see Jane.

"Abe Terrill, it's so good to see you," Jane told him.

"Ma'm, I'm sorry that I don't have word from your husband," Abe told her. "But when I get to Matamoros, I'll do everything I can to find out something for you. I'll write you at once if I learn anything. Someone coming this way will bring you the letter."

With that promise, Jane's hopes rose. Her heart felt much lighter. Abe Terrill would be sure to find out something about James Long.

In March, James Smith came back in the little pirogue.

"Mrs. Long, I have come back for you. You must return to San Jacinto with us," James Smith told her.

"Jane, you must come home with us," Peggy Smith begged. "You just can't stay here like this any longer."

Jane looked around her. Bolivar had been her

home for more than a year. This was the place where James Long had left her. He had said that he would be back. As he had told her to do, she had guarded the fort alone for months.

Tears came to Jane's eyes as she thought about leaving. How would James know where to find her? Her feelings were mixed. She knew that her babies and Kian deserved a better life than she could give them here. They had lived through hardships that were beyond imagination.

Sadly, she made up her mind to leave. She looked back on the fort with mixed feelings. She had been happy there with James. It was to have been their home.

"I suppose James will find me, if I stay in Texas," she told the Smiths. "Perhaps someone will tell him that I am at San Jacinto."

They rowed slowly up the bay toward the San Jacinto River. The dog Galveston followed them along the shore. The faithful dog would not be left behind. Jane knew that he would follow the boat. She watched eagerly for glimpses of him trotting along. At least Galveston was happy with the turn of events.

They reached the Smiths' home sometime in April. Jane was sad about leaving Point Bolivar, but she was glad to be with people again. However, her happiness was not to last long.

Life was not pleasant at the Smiths. The family was unhappy. There was much quarreling and bickering. Although Peggy Smith was pleasant around Jane, the others made her feel that her living there was a bother to them. Finally, James Smith became ill. While the fever consumed his body, the family was not very good to him. Jane felt that they neglected him.

"I feel so sorry for the poor man. He suffers so

much," she told one of her visitors.

When James Smith died, Jane knew that she would have to make some other plans. The Rankin family had given her some assistance. So she decided to move closer to them.

An old Negro man came to visit her at the Rankins' home. He planned to help Jane Long.

"Ma'm, your husband was good to me. I want to help you," he said.

"Thank you so much," Jane told him. "I appreciate any help you can give me. My husband will be very grateful to you."

The old man built a crude hut for Jane out of palmetto leaves and boards that he had salvaged. The hut was rude and rough, but to Jane it was beautiful. It was a home. There she did not have to depend upon anyone else.

Sometimes a visitor would bring her some venison. She spent her days fishing in the little bayou. She planted a little garden. Life was not really good, but it was certainly more pleasant than life had been at the Smiths.

It was here that Randall Jones and his brother James found her. She recognized him immediately as he rode up. Jane ran toward his horse, throwing her arms up to him.

"I am so glad to see you, Randall," she cried.

"Jane Long, I thought I'd never find you," he told her. "I went by the fort, but there was no one there."

"My husband?" she cried.

Randall Jones lowered his eyes as he answered her.

"Jane, I'm so sorry to have to tell you. James Long isn't coming back," he said. "Dear Jane, life has been so hard on you. I wish I could spare you this news."

"But, Randall, what is it? Can't you tell me?" Jane begged. She knew now that it was going to be bad, but she had to know.

"He was killed in Mexico City. His enemies had him shot. He was a prisoner on parole. They arranged to rid themselves of him," Jones told her.

The woman of courage stared into the distance. Then slowly she slipped to the ground in a faint. Her James was never coming back to her.

IV

Life Goes On

Jane Long sat in her little cabin, thinking of the past days. It did not seem possible that James Long was dead. She remembered the happy plans that they had made. This had to be only a bad dream. Then she knew that it was not a dream. It was real.

Kian and Ann tried to ease her pain and grief. They tiptoed around the house. They spoke softly to her. Days passed, and somehow the pain began to go away.

"Kian, bring me my writing case," Jane called. "I must write to my sister Barbara. I have to tell her about my plans."

"Yes, Ma'm," Kian answered. "I'll get it out right now."

The devoted Kian was happy with this news. Perhaps Miss Jane could get started to living again. It had seemed that she never would. Ever since Randall Jones had arrived, Jane had been so very sad.

"I think perhaps I should make plans to go to San Antonio. James would want me to do that. The government should give help to the general's family," Jane told Randall Jones when he came to see her the next day.

A few days later Ann and Kian were out in the garden picking late beans. A sharp sound made them look up. Down the lane came a black man riding a huge mule. He reined in the mule when he saw the two women picking beans. He tipped his worn hat to Ann as she walked toward him.

Please, young Miss, can you tell me where I can find Mis' Jane Long?" he asked of Ann.

Ann answered him pleasantly in a teasing voice, "I certainly can. She is my mother, and she is in the cabin yonder."

The man said, "Well, I thank you, Miss Ann. and I imagine you're Kian?" He turned his gaze toward Kian.

"You imagine right!" Kian answered him sharply. She did not like to be taken for granted this way. This was an uppity black man!

"I am Tom, Mis' Long's new man. The Calvits sent me to help her. I brought this mule for her, too," the man went on. He ignored Kian's sharp answer. He smiled at her as he turned the mule toward the cabin door.

"I'll call Mama," Ann told him. She ran around the rows, dropping the already picked beans from her apron as she ran.

Kian muttered after her, "Look at the work we've wasted, Missy. Now I'll have to go along picking them up off the ground."

Tom got off the mule and knocked on the cabin door. He smiled at Jane when she opened it.

"Mis' Jane, I'se Tom. The Calvits sent me to you. I have a letter here for you. Mis' Calvit said I should give it to you in person," Tom told Jane as he handed her the letter.

"I thank you, Tom. We certainly do need your help. I'm so glad Mrs. Calvit sent you," Jane said. She opened the letter and read it quickly. Then she called to Kian and Ann.

"Kian, you can start getting our things together," she said. "We are going to San Antonio. My sister agrees with me that I should ask Trespalacios for help. I know he will try to do something for us."

On September 9, 1822, Jane Long set out for San Antonio. She rode a horse and carried Mary James in her arms. Little Ann rode the big pack mule that Tom had brought. Randall and James Jones shared a horse between them. The Negroes, including Kian and Tom, walked along after the party. As soon as they found a place where the game was plentiful, they stopped for over a week. The time was spent in killing and drying beef and venison for the trip. Thus they prepared for the hard journey.

The trip was very hard on Mary James. She developed a high fever. They had much trouble in finding enough water. At times the horses and mules almost died for lack of water.

At the first cabin they found, Jane suggested that they rest for awhile so that Mary James could get well. The kindly farmer gave them a powder keg to carry water in.

"Ma'm, that baby just has to have some good water. She's going to die if you don't take better care of her," the farmer told Jane.

"Thank you, sir. We are grateful for your help," Jane said. "I certainly do intend to take good care of my baby." She had the keg tied on behind her saddle. The others might have to do without, but Mary James would have fresh water. Jane would see to that.

That night they stopped by a river crossing. Two men who were camped there told them that they had better spend the night by the river. The

Karankawas were out on the prairie in front of them. Jane was frightened by the Indians, but she refused to stay. Jane was right as it turned out. The two men were found murdered the next day. The Indians had returned to the river that night.

When Jane's party arrived at Goliad, they were well treated. The townspeople decided to give a ball in honor of General Long's widow.

"But, Randall, I can't attend a ball. I am in mourning for my husband," Jane said when Randall told her of the invitation.

"Jane, you must go. These people will feel hurt. They are doing this because of your husband's work," said Randall. "It will surely be all right for you to watch the party."

The people respected Jane's wishes. However, when the priest asked Jane to dance, everyone insisted that she dance. And dance she did. James would not have objected to her dancing. Jane knew that. Jane's natural love for people had won her over. From this time on she began her return to life as she had once known it.

It was five weeks after leaving San Jacinto that Jane and her party arrived in San Antonio. It had been a long trip, and they were all tired. They went first to the Alamo, the fort on the east side of the river.

After dinner, Randall told Jane that he and his brother James would arrange for her to see Trespalacios.

"We'll go to see Baron Felipe Enrique Neri de Bastrop. He can get us in to see Trespalacios. I have known the baron for many years," Randall said.

"I hope he can arrange my visit with the man. I remember that James did not trust Trespalacios. However, perhaps he will help me now," Jane answered.

Baron de Bastrop did go with them. Trespalacios answered their request with a quick invitation to Jane. When she came, he bowed low over her hand as he kissed it.

"Ma'm, please accept my sincere sympathy for the death of your husband. He was a fine soldier and a gallant soldier," Trespalacios told Jane.

"Thank you, sir. You are very kind," Jane said. She watched him carefully. He was polite, but James had told her that kind manners could hide evil doings. Jane was not at all sure of Trespalacios.

"I have arranged for you to stay in the home of Don Erasmo Seguin," Trespalacios told her. "They will make you very comfortable in their home."

Jane was grateful for his help. Before long, she was able to arrange an apartment in the Seguin home. There she would make a little home for her family. But life was not to remain calm for long. Trespalacios began to make plans to go to Monterrey. He urged Jane to go with him.

"Mrs. Long, you can be sure that the Mexican government will help you. They are grateful for your husband's service. But they must know about your problems first," he said. "If you go to Monterrey, the officials there will inform the government in Mexico City of your need."

Jane could not make up her mind. She thought that it would just be another mistake. After all, it was such a long trip. The babies were not up to such travel. However, she could not live with the Seguin family forever. She must have some help.

It was just at this time that another kind figure came to Jane's aid. Leonard Peck, a Philadelphia merchant, came to San Antonio. He had heard of Jane's difficulties. Since he was on his way to Monterrey, he offered to take Jane and her family with him.

"Mrs. Long, I can see that you get there safely. I will be happy to help you," said Mr. Peck. "I think that the Mexican government will indeed give you some aid. After all they owe your dead husband a great debt."

"Thank you, Mr. Peck," Jane answered. "I value your kind offer."

Before they left for Monterrey, Jane's friends in San Antonio told her that Mary James should be christened. It was unthinkable that she had not had it done already.

"Jane, I have a long, white christening robe that you may use," said one lady. "I will see that it is laundered and prepared nicely for the ceremony."

Another friend arranged for a procession to carry the baby across town to the church. Along the way, friends tossed over a hundred dollars in silver coins to the poor. When the ceremony was over, they returned to Jane's apartment where they showered the baby with gifts. It was a happy occasion for all the family.

"I cannot thank you kind people enough for all these lovely gifts. It was such a sweet ceremony for Mary James. I am sure that when she grows up, she will always carry a deep feeling for the people of San Antonio," Jane told her guests.

After Jane had rested in Monterrey, she finally undertook the long journey to Mexico City. She felt that she must visit her husband's grave.

Although Kian insisted that she would go with Jane to visit James Long's grave, Jane went by herself. In her arms she carried a bouquet of bright-hued flowers. She stood alone by his grave. A soft wind blew over the hill at Chapultepec. She gazed down at the creek around the foot of the hill. Her tears flowed down her cheeks like the waters in the creek.

Then suddenly it seemed that she could face life again. The memory of James Long gave her strength. Jane made up her mind to pay back every debt that darkened his name. She would work to clear everything against his name. As she placed the flowers on the grave, she was aware of another mourner beside her. When she turned to look at him, he spoke to her softly.

"Jane, I know what great sorrow you bear today," Ben Milam's voice came to her. "I have come to take you back to Texas. James Long wanted me to take care of you."

"Thank you, Ben Milam. I am thankful that my husband had friends like you," Jane answered him.

"James talked with me the night before he died," Ben Milam continued to say. "He wanted me always to be a brother to you and a father to his child. I shall do my very best to fulfill his request. I will protect you and your children with my life!"

"Ben Milam, you are a wonderful and loyal friend," Jane said with tears in her eyes. She took his hand and together they walked back down the hill to the carriage that had brought her to Chapultepec.

Ben Milam kept his promise to James Long. He faithfully helped Jane Long until his death in 1835. He died in the fighting around San Antonio.

Although Jane had been promised payment for her husband's great service, she never received the eleven leagues of land. For awhile she returned to Louisiana to visit her sister, Mrs. Calvit. However, she was not happy there. For one thing, little Mary James died in the summer of 1824. After much talk, Mrs. Calvit and her family agreed to emigrate to Texas with Jane.

With the Calvit family's promise to follow her soon, Jane left Louisiana. She went to the home of

Colonel Jared E. Groce. She remained on the Groce Plantation for nearly a year. Then the Calvit family arrived to make their new home.

Shortly after her return to Texas, Jane Long had learned the extent of the debts she would have to pay. But the big blow came when she learned about Kian. Kian had been mortgaged to a creditor. The man foreclosed on the debt and took Kian away from Jane.

Tearfully, Jane bade Kian good-bye.

"Kian, I promise you. I will bring you back to my family some way," she told the crying Kian.

Jane went to work tirelessly to redeem Kian from bondage. With the help of an old friend from Natchez, she was able to buy Kian and bring her back home. Jane and Kian established a boarding house at Brazoria. Kian did the duties required in caring for the boarders. Later she and Jane maintained another boarding house in Richmond, Texas. They ran a farm on land granted to Jane by the Republic of Texas. All of James Long's debts were finally repaid.

Jane Long never remarried. Although she had many suitors, her heart lay buried with her soldier husband in Mexico. She died in Richmond, Texas, when she was eighty-two years old. At her side when she died were her many friends and grandchildren. There was also another Kian, the granddaughter of the faithful woman who had been her servant, friend, and companion through the years. On December 30, 1880, Jane Long was buried in a peaceful little cemetery at Richmond, Texas, under a simple stone marker. But the memory of a woman of courage lives on.

BIBLIOGRAPHY

Atteck, J.D., "Passages in the Life of Mrs. Jane Herbert Long . . . " *Galveston Daily News,* 25 March 1881, p. 2.

Brindley, Anne A., "Jane Long," *Southwestern Historical Quarterly,* Vol. 56, pp. 211-238.

Dobie, J. Frank, "Story of Jane Long, Evangeline of Texas," *Galveston Daily News,* 11 April 1942, pp. 6-B.

Garwood, Ellen, "A Study in Social Relationships," *Southwestern Historical Quarterly,* Vol. 60, pp. 219-230.

Hunter, Theresa M., *Romantic Interludes,* "Another Evangline," San Antonio, The Naylor Company, 1936.

"Jane Wikinson Long . . . ," *Galveston Tribune Magazine Section,* 9 February 1929.

"Lady's Lonely Vigil," *The Galveston Daily News,* 13 Jan. 1907.

Syers, Ed, "Old Bolivar Lighthouse Marks Jane Long's Lonely Vigil," *San Antonio Express/News,* 20 Oct 1963.

Ziegler, Jesse A., " 'Mother of Texas' Courageous Woman," *The Houston Post,* 6 June 1937.